About This Book

Title: *Ice*

Step: 4

Word Count: 199

Skills in Focus: Silent e

Tricky Words: water, cold, forms, freezes, kinds, winter, snow, tray, indoor, outside

Ideas For Using This Book

Before Reading:

- **Comprehension:** Look at the title and cover image together. Ask readers what they know about ice. What new things do they think they might learn in the book?
- **Accuracy:** Practice saying the tricky words listed on page 1.
- **Phonics:** Look at the title and write the word *ice* on a piece of paper. Point to the pattern *i_e* in the word. Explain that the silent *e* makes the vowel before it have a long sound, saying its own name, /i/. Remind readers that the *c* in the word is soft because it's followed by an *e*. Model how to say each sound in the word *ice* slowly in isolation. Then, blend the sounds together smoothly to say the whole word. Offer additional examples from the book, such as *slide, like, cube, place, lake, skate, blade,* and *nice*.

During Reading:

- Have readers point under each word as they read it.
- **Decoding:** If readers are stuck on a word, help them say each sound and blend the sounds together smoothly. After reading a sentence, point out words with silent *e* as they appear.
- **Comprehension:** Invite readers to talk about new things they are learning about ice while reading. What are they learning that they didn't know before?

After Reading:

Discuss the book. Some ideas for questions:

- What are some places where you can find ice?
- What are some different forms of ice?

Ice

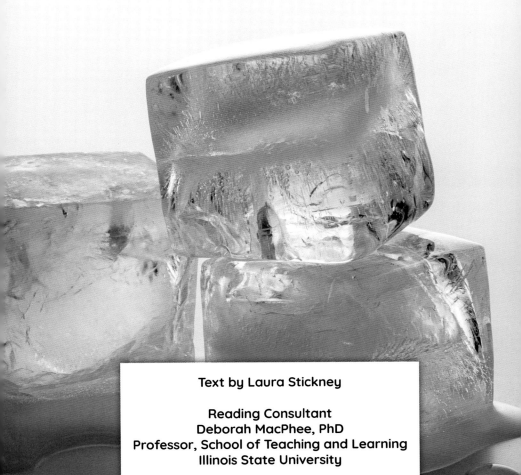

Text by Laura Stickney

Reading Consultant
Deborah MacPhee, PhD
Professor, School of Teaching and Learning
Illinois State University

PICTURE WINDOW BOOKS
a capstone imprint

What Is Ice?
Ice forms when water freezes.

Water freezes when it gets cold. The cold makes it a solid.

Ice can take lots of forms. It can be white. Or it can be like glass.

Ice shines in the sun.
Snow and frost are kinds of ice.

Ice melts when a place gets hot.

When ice melts, it changes back into water.

Ice in Winter

In winter, ice forms on places like paths.

You can slip and slide on this slick ice.

Lakes freeze in the cold too. Ice forms on the lakes.

You can skate on it.

Slide on skates with blades.

Lace up the skates.

Skates help you glide and race on the ice.

On a lake, do not skate where there is thin ice. It can crack in these places.

You can also skate at ice rinks. These are cold indoor spaces with ice.

People made this ice for skating.

Ice Cubes

Ice is nice when it is hot outside.

You can freeze water to make ice cubes.

Place water in a tray.

Then place the tray in a freezer.

Plop ice cubes in your lemonade to make it nice and chill.

More Ideas:

Phonics and Phonemic Awareness Activity

Practicing Silent *e*:
Play I Spy! Prepare word cards with silent *e* story words. Place each card face up on a surface. Choose a word to start the game. Break apart the sounds and say, "I spy /i/, /c/" (segment word of choice). The readers will call out the word and then look for the corresponding card. Continue until all cards have been collected. For an extra challenge, have students be the caller, choosing and breaking apart a word.

Suggested words: ice, make, skate, blade, glide, race, lace, lake, shine, cube

Extended Learning Activity

Ice Experiment:
Help readers fill an ice cube tray or another container with water. Ask them to write a sentence about what the water in the tray looks like. Then put the tray in the freezer. Once the water has frozen into ice cubes, take the tray out of the freezer and have students study the cubes. Ask them to write another sentence describing how the water has changed. Challenge readers to use silent *e* words in their sentences.

Published by Picture Window Books, an imprint of Capstone
1710 Roe Crest Drive, North Mankato, Minnesota 56003
capstonepub.com

Copyright © 2026 by Capstone.
All rights reserved. No part of this publication may be reproduced in whole or in part, or stored in a retrieval system, or transmitted in any form or by any means, electronic, mechanical, photocopying, recording, or otherwise, without written permission of the publisher.

Library of Congress Cataloging-in-Publication Data is available on the Library of Congress website.

ISBN: 9798875227158 (hardback)
ISBN: 9798875230646 (paperback)
ISBN: 9798875230622 (eBook PDF)

Image Credits: iStock: Anna Perfilova, 17, FatCamera, 16, 30, mammoth, 8–9, sundown001, 14, szefei, 24, xphotoz, 5; Shutterstock: 3445128471, 1, 28–29, Branislav Nenin, 15, DardaInna, 22–23, Friday_Ahlis, 4, Joeri Mostmans, 10–11, Lloyd Carr, 20–21, Lukassek, 12–13, New Africa, 25, Olga Dubravina, 26–27, r.classen, 2–3, Scott Latham, 6, Standret, cover, Svitlyk, 7, Tomsickova Tatyana, 18–19, 32

Printed and bound in China. 6274